HOW TO CREAT

A

MARKETING STRATEGY

The Ultimate Guide to Crafting a Magnetic
Marketing Strategy.

LYNNE RUFFIN

Table of content

Introduction

A key element in predicting your success in the fast-paced world of business is your ability to understand the essence of your company and its place in the market. By using this crucial information as a guide, strategic choices and actions may be made with more efficiency. In the course of this investigation, we look at the fundamental elements that make up a company, with a focus on how important it is to understand both the internal dynamics and the exterior market rivalry.

The Foundation: Understanding Your Business and Market

Recognize the dynamics that exist inside you.

The foundation of every effective business strategy is a thorough comprehension of the dynamics that occur inside the company. To do this, one must have a thorough understanding of the mission, vision, values, and objectives of the company. This is similar to knowing the ins and outs of your team, infrastructure, and operations, as well as having a thorough map of the terrain you go through.

- **Goals, guiding concepts, and declarations of intent**

These essential elements define the goal and strategy of your business. They serve as guiding principles for decision-making by outlining the what, how, and why. Implementing tactics that align with the organization's mission, vision, and values guarantees a purposeful and cohesive approach.

- **A SWOT analysis**

A SWOT analysis, or strengths, weaknesses, opportunities, and threats, is a helpful tool for internal evaluation. By recognizing internal strengths to build upon, weaknesses to address, chances to seize, and dangers to mitigate, businesses may make well-informed choices.

- **Dynamics of Teams**

Employees are an organization's most valuable asset. In an atmosphere where team dynamics, communication preferences, and individual abilities are recognized, productivity and collaboration are increased. Investing in the growth and well-being of employees has a significant impact on the overall success of a firm.

Understanding the Market: External Factors

In addition to its internal dynamics, a firm operates within a larger ecosystem that is impacted by external market circumstances. To survive, one must be able to identify and react to these outside dynamics.

- **Market Analysis**

Undertaking thorough market research is necessary to comprehend external forces. This includes analyzing consumer behavior, rivalry tactics, market trends, and industry advances. With this knowledge, businesses can identify flaws, anticipate changes, and make wise decisions.

- **The Environment of Competition**

It's crucial to evaluate opponents in-depth. Learning about their strengths and weaknesses may help you differentiate your business. It also makes it possible to identify unexplored business niches and potential joint venture possibilities.

- **The Regulation Environment**

The regulatory landscape significantly impacts how businesses operate. By staying up to date with industry standards and compliance regulations, you can ensure that your business operates legally and reduce the risks associated with non-compliance.

Coordination: Connecting the Inward and Outer Domains

The true value of knowing the foundation lies in its capacity to seamlessly link one's own strengths with external opportunities. To do this, the company must be positioned for long-term development and its internal resources must be in line with market needs.

- **Strategic Planning**

Armed with data from evaluations conducted both internally and outside, strategy planning becomes a dynamic process. Businesses may set reasonable goals supported by a plan that accounts for both internal resources and external market conditions.

- **Originality and Adaptability**

Flexibility makes a huge impact in the ever-changing corporate climate. Organizations may remain ahead of the curve by fostering a creative culture. Flexibility is essential for long-term success and may be attained via product innovation, process optimization, or the use of cutting-edge technology.

- **Continuous Evaluation and Adjustment**

The structure of the foundation is dynamic. It has to be constantly checked and adjusted. Regularly reviewing internal and external evaluations ensures that the company stays flexible and adaptable to shifting market conditions.

Understanding your organization's basis essentially entails paying equal attention to internal dynamics and external market factors. Comprehending the unique characteristics of your company and staying current with the ever-changing market landscape will enable your business to surmount obstacles and capitalize on opportunities. Using this fundamental idea as a guide for making strategic decisions, businesses may be resilient and sustainable in the face of competition.

Chapter One

Market Research

In the fast-paced world of business, market research is essential to strategic planning and informed decision-making. The main goals of this challenging procedure, which involves investigating several points of view, are to gather vital information about the intended audience and to assess the level of competition. In addition to revealing consumer preferences and demands, this research equips businesses with all the knowledge they need to navigate the competitive landscape and outmaneuver rival tactics.

Gathering Key Insights on Target Audience

Analyzing the tastes and behavior of the target audience is similar to figuring out the consumer behavior issue. This portion of market research is essential for businesses looking to tailor their goods and services to the specific requirements of their clientele.

- **Demographic Profiling**

Developing a demographic profile is essential to understanding your target market. The audience has to be categorized based on age, gender, income, education, and other crucial factors in order to do this. This kind of data provides a broad picture of the consumer, which helps in the construction of targeted marketing campaigns.

Analyzing Psychographic Information

Understanding the values, interests, way of

life, and attitudes of the target audience is necessary to conduct a more thorough psychographic study. This goes beyond simple demographic data by providing insights into the psychological and emotional factors influencing purchasing choices.

- **Behavior Patterns**

Examining trends in behavior may provide important information about how consumers use goods and services. This include examining consumer behavior, product use, and brand loyalty. These kinds of data help businesses enhance their offerings in order to meet the needs and expectations of their customers.

- **Feedback Mechanisms**

Finding and analyzing consumer input on a regular basis is a vital part of knowing your target market. Social media interactions, reviews, and polls may provide businesses with current information on the preferences, anxieties, and satisfaction levels of their customers.

Analyzing Competitor Landscape

A strong market research strategy includes a thorough analysis of the competitive environment in addition to determining the target audience. It is necessary to thoroughly investigate competitors' businesses to identify their strengths, weaknesses, opportunities, and dangers in order to develop a strategic advantage.

Comparing yourself to competitors

Benchmarking is the process of comparing key performance metrics with those of other companies. Examples of this include price plans, product features, expectations for customer service, and market share.

Identifying the company's advantages and disadvantages provides a path for future strategic developments.

- **Competitors' SWOT analysis**

Companies use a SWOT analysis for internal evaluations, and using the same framework to analyze rivals works quite well. While identifying a competitor's strengths encourages uniqueness, identifying their shortcomings allows for more strategic maneuvering options.

- **Positioning in the Industry**

Assessing the way rivals set up shop in the industry is essential. This entails looking at USPs, branding strategies, and target audience appeal. Businesses may use this information to establish a unique niche for themselves or to improve their market standing.

- **Novel Advancements and Patterns**

By closely monitoring changes in the industrial environment, businesses may predict future trends and technological advances. This kind of foresight makes it possible for businesses to react to changes in the market or in technology, which helps them remain competitive.

Integration to Make Knowledgeable Choices

When market research integrates the knowledge gained from studying rivals with an understanding of the target market, it flourishes. Businesses may use these crucial information to inform decisions across a variety of operational domains.

Product Development and Innovation: Businesses that possess a thorough understanding of the demands and preferences of their target market are better equipped to create and manufacture goods and services that appeal to that market. Insights from competition research also guarantee that the products are distinct in the marketplace.

Strategies for Marketing and Communication:

Tailoring marketing and communication techniques to the preferences and values of the target audience improves engagement. Organizations that fully understand competition strategy may also successfully distinguish their message.

Strategic planning and risk mitigation:

Well-informed strategic planning takes into account both internal capabilities and the dynamics of the external market. Organizations may effectively manage risks, seize opportunities, and strategically position themselves in the market by combining insights from target audience analysis with competitive landscape research.

Market research serves as a compass to help businesses negotiate the intricacies of the competitive landscape. Companies set themselves up for success by carefully collecting crucial information about their target market and doing in-depth market analysis. This two-pronged approach guarantees that decisions are made with a thorough understanding of the market dynamics rather than in a vacuum. In order for businesses to be competitive, adaptable, and aware of market and industry trends while navigating the ever-changing business environment, market research is still an essential tool.

Chapter Two

Defining Your Unique Value Proposition

One of the key ideas in the complex field of marketing strategy that may make or break a company is the concept of a Unique Value Proposition (UVP). What sets a business apart from the competition and provides consumers with a strong reason to choose one product or service over another is its unique value proposition, or UVP. In this study, we explore the nuances of developing a unique value proposition, emphasizing the need of identifying your company's unique selling points and crafting a message that appeals to your target audience.

What Sets Your Business Apart

Understanding what makes your business different from the competition is the cornerstone of the Unique Value Proposition. This necessitates a thorough examination of every material and intangible element that makes your company special.

Key Competencies and Differentiators:

Identify the essential skills that set your company apart. This might be unique technology, a specific set of skills, excellent customer service, or anything else that makes you stand apart. An effective UVP starts with an understanding of and use of key differentiators.

A client-centered strategy:

An effective customer-centric strategy requires a thorough understanding of both your product or service and the needs and problems of your target market. Tailoring your products and services to specifically meet the needs of your consumers increases their perceived value and presents your business as one that really values and knows its customers.

Adaptability and Creativity:

Businesses that innovate and adapt to shifting market conditions often have a significant advantage. An appealing UVP may be achieved by showcasing your company's capacity to remain ahead of the curve via innovative products, cutting-edge services, or nimble business procedures.

Crafting a compelling Message

The next crucial stage is to turn these unique qualities of your business into a compelling message that appeals to your target audience. To create a UVP message, one must be exact, concise, and proficient in the emotional cues that influence the decisions made by clients.

- **Clarity and Simplicity**

A powerful UVP message must be understandable, succinct, and unambiguous. Avoid using jargon or technical terms that might mislead prospective customers. When your message is concise and easy to understand, it becomes simpler to recall and share your distinct value.

- **Resolving Customer Complains**

A strong UVP addresses the challenges and issues that your intended audience is facing. By emphasizing how your product or service meets a need or addresses a particular issue, you establish a direct line of communication with clients and position your business as a suitable substitute.

- **Making an emotional appeal**

Appealing to the emotions of your audience makes your UVP more successful than just functional. Understanding and using emotional triggers into your message—be they security, belonging, or desire—will help you build stronger relationships with your clients.

- **Differentiating from competitors**

Clearly state how your company is different from competitors in a manner that will captivate your audience. This might be touting unique qualities, impressive features, a better customized experience, or anything else that gives your business an advantage over competitors.

Real-World Examples of Effective UVPs

Examining real-world company case studies with compelling value propositions reveals a range of strategies and the power of a well-crafted message.

- **"Think Different" is the tagline for Apple.**

Apple places a strong emphasis on design, innovation, and nonconformity. The "Think Different" campaign not only draws attention to how unique Apple products are, but it also presents the company as a symbol of creativity and innovation.

- **Volvo "For Life"**

Safety is the cornerstone of Volvo's UVP. When making decisions about what to buy, consumers who value safety are motivated by a brand's unwavering commitment to producing safe cars.

- **Dollar Shave Club's tagline is "Shave Time. Shave Money."**

Dollar Shave Club revolutionized the razor industry by providing an affordable, high-quality membership service. The UVP is easy to understand and has time- and money-saving features that make it appealing to a wide range of people.

Incorporation into Marketing Strategy

Rather than standing alone, the UVP is a pillar that is included into the larger marketing plan. Your UVP will be more effective if it is coordinated with other marketing initiatives and ensures that the message is conveyed consistently across media.

❖ **Branding and Visual Identity**

The visual identity of your brand need to align with the UVP. Each visual element—such as color schemes and logos—should convey the unique value proposition and produce a recognizable and cohesive brand image.

❖ **Content Promotion**

Content marketing is a really powerful tool that you may use to improve UVP. Enhance my writing style and increase my UVP by using success stories, industry insights, and instructional material that highlights the unique qualities of your product or service.

❖ **Customer input and engagement:**

Make a concerted effort to get customer feedback and participate in order to validate and improve your UVP. Case studies, evaluations, and customer endorsements all be helpful resources to show real-world instances of how your company delivers on its unique value offer.

Developing a distinctive value proposition is a challenging process that demands a thorough understanding of both the distinctive qualities of your company and the needs of your target market. To create an engaging message that makes your company stand out, you need to combine emotional appeal, differentiation from rivals, problem-solving for customers, and clarity. Your marketing approach may be propelled by a well-defined unique value proposition (UVP), which may help establish your brand, establish a connection with consumers, and cultivate enduring loyalty. Companies may create a long-lasting impression on the market by using the Unique Value Proposition as a beacon to help them navigate the competitive environment.

Chapter Three

Setting Marketing Objectives

A key to success in the dynamic field of marketing strategy is establishing precise, well-defined goals. This involves using SMART objectives—which stand for Specific, Measurable, Achievable, Relevant, and Time-bound—in order to provide an ordered and focused approach. It is essential to connect these marketing goals with the company's overarching vision in order to further ensure that marketing initiatives support the larger strategic direction. This question addresses the nuances of goal-setting in marketing, emphasizing the value of SMART targets and how well they align with the overall business strategy.

SMART Goals for Strategic Focus

Specific: Preciseness in Goal

Setting goals is the cornerstone of a successful marketing plan. To do this, the objectives must be clearly stated and every possibility of misinterpretation must be eliminated. A more specific goal may be, for instance, "increase online sales by 20% within the next quarter," as opposed to a more general goal like "increase sales." This accuracy provides a clear direction, ensuring that efforts are focused and resources are allocated appropriately.

Measurable: Determine Success

Measurability is essential for tracking development and evaluating the effectiveness of marketing campaigns. A measurable aim is one that can be quantified and evaluated in a way that makes sense. If increasing brand recognition is the goal, a quantifiable figure may be, for example, a percentage increase in website visits or social media activity. By tracking results, marketers are able to adjust their tactics in real time and make well-informed judgments.

Realistic: Justifiable and Attainable Goals

While desire is admirable, maintaining motivation and ensuring significant results depend on achieving realistic objectives. The goals need to push the team while being grounded in reality. Excessively high aspirations may cause suffering, yet low aspirations may not have the same motivating power necessary for advancement. Achieving the right mix makes marketing initiatives difficult but doable.

Important: Consistency with the Overarching Plan

What makes everything relevant is making sure that marketing objectives align with the organization's broader strategic goals. The effectiveness of the whole plan is instantly impacted by a well defined aim. For example, if the goal of the firm is to increase the number of customers it serves, then targeting a certain demographic or geographic area might be a useful marketing goal. This synergy guarantees that marketing initiatives have a significant impact on the company's development trajectory.

Time-bound: Creating a Detailed Timetable

A time-bound aim creates a feeling of urgency by providing a deadline for completing tasks. A schedule helps with the long-term or short-term planning and implementation of any strategy. For instance, setting a target to launch a new product and achieve a certain market share during the next six months gives the marketing team a specific timeline to strive towards.

Aligning Objectives with Business Vision

Vision is the North Star

The firm vision guides and directs every organizational endeavor. Marketing objectives should be inextricably linked to this broader vision in order to ensure that every marketing action contributes to the achievement of the larger company goals. If the firm would want to become a leader in sustainable practices, then marketing goals that focus on CSR or the promotion of environmentally friendly products might be pursued.

Standardization Across Departments

All departments inside the company, not only the marketing department, must be consistent in order to be in line with the corporate goal. Collaborating across divisions is essential to ensuring that the whole company works as a unit to achieve common goals, from product development to customer service. This cross-functional alignment increases the effectiveness of marketing techniques in achieving the overall corporate purpose.

Customer-focused objectives

Usually, the main objectives of a firm are to satisfy customers and create value. Marketing goals should reflect this client-centric approach by emphasizing customer happiness, understanding their preferences, and fostering enduring connections. If, for instance, the corporate vision places a high value on customer loyalty, then marketing goals may include developing loyalty programs or using specific communication techniques.

Versatility and Adjustment

While congruence is important, it's also critical to recognize that organizational settings are dynamic. Marketing goals should be flexible enough to accommodate emerging trends, shifting consumer preferences, and unanticipated obstacles. Regular reviews and adjustments guarantee that marketing initiatives stay aligned with the ever-changing business goal.

Matching the Overarching Vision with Key Performance Indicators (KPIs)

Choosing pertinent Key Performance Indicators (KPIs) is essential for tracking progress toward marketing goals and, therefore, the overarching vision of the business. KPIs must be chosen based on how well they support the main objective. For instance, the KPIs may include measures for foreign market penetration, client acquisition in new nations, or improved brand awareness worldwide if the company's goal is global growth.

Establishing marketing goals is a strategic process that requires precision, lucidity, and alignment with the larger business strategy. Marketing teams may navigate the complexities of the market with purpose and concentration by establishing SMART objectives since they guarantee a measured and focused approach. When these goals align with the business's corporate strategy, a coherent framework is created where every marketing initiative significantly contributes to the success of the firm as a whole. As firms adapt and take on new challenges, the relationship between SMART objectives and the corporate vision remains a dynamic force driving them toward sustainable development and success in the competitive market.

Chapter Four

Target Audience Segmentation

When it comes to marketing strategy, target audience segmentation is similar to tuning an instrument to produce the most beautiful music. By carefully identifying and comprehending distinct client groups, the method enables businesses to modify their messaging so that they effectively connect with a wide range of customers. This investigation examines the nuances of target audience segmentation, emphasizing the need of identifying discrete client groups and developing messages that specifically address their specific needs and interests.

Identifying and Understanding Customer Segments

Demographic Segmentation: Going Beyond Basic Categories.

Classifying the target population based on observable variables such as age, gender, income, employment, and educational attainment is known as demographic segmentation. Nevertheless, in the ever-changing world of marketing today, it's essential to go beyond simple demographics. The segmentation method provides a deeper understanding of the audience, which is further supported by information about the values, way of life, and behavioral patterns linked to certain demographic groups.

For example, a skincare company targeting women in their 30s may delve further into the lifestyle decisions, preferred beauty regimens, and skincare opinions of these women in order to develop more customized and relevant marketing strategies.

Examining Psychographic Segmentation to Find Motives and Preferences.

Psychographic segmentation examines the psychological aspects of customer behavior. It is essential for this to comprehend the beliefs, passions, attitudes, and lifestyle preferences of the target audience. Knowing what influences consumer choices may help businesses create messages that more deeply and emotionally connect with their target audience.

Consider a fitness company that caters to psychographic groups in addition to basic demographics like those who like working out. Some clients may be driven by a need for privacy and a personal challenge, while others may be driven by a need for community and social interaction (group fitness courses) (individual exercise routines).

Using Behavioral Segmentation to Examine Behavior and Interactions.

The measurement of consumers' behavior, buying habits, and reactions to various stimuli is the foundation of behavioral segmentation. It necessitates understanding the advantages consumers want, their steadfast brand loyalty, and their receptivity to trying out new products or services. By using this segmentation technique, a business may more effectively target its marketing messages based on how its clients engage with it.

An e-commerce platform could classify customers according to factors like past purchases, shopping habits, and responsiveness to promotions. Frequent buyers could get special loyalty offers, while infrequent buyers might be targeted with incentives to promote interaction.

Geographic Division: Contextualization of Message.

Geographic segmentation creates a framework for localizing communications by dividing the target audience based on their geography. For businesses operating in multicultural, multiethnic, or multiclimatic markets, this strategy is very important.

For instance, a multinational retailer of clothing may alter its marketing vocabulary to correspond with local seasonal variations. While campaigns with a winter theme could target consumers in colder locations, those with a summer theme might be more appropriate for clients in warmer climes.

Tailoring Messages to Different Audiences

Personalization: Exceeding Just Putting a Name on It.

Customization in marketing today goes beyond just adding a customer's name to an email. These days, creating communications that really relate to people's interests and behaviors is necessary. Organizations may create highly tailored communications that are relevant and compelling by using customer interaction data.

For example, an online streaming service may look into a user's viewing habits and preferences in order to provide material that is relevant to their particular interests. This level of personalization improves the consumer experience and fosters loyalty.

Customizing Content Formats: Meeting Various Needs.

Different client groups may absorb information in different forms. While some readers may read longer, more in-depth texts, others could interact better with visual content. To tailor their message to certain audiences, businesses might alter content formats to fit their tastes.

Imagine a tech company presenting a fresh product idea. While a tech-savvy industry would prefer lengthy whitepapers and specs, a less tech-savvy audience could prefer video demos showcasing the product's user-friendly features.

Customized Promotions and Awards: Fulfilling Specific Needs.

Promotions and incentives tailored to different client segments take into account their unique needs and motivators. One method of doing this would be to provide each group with exclusive access, discounts, or loyalty rewards that align with their preferences and lifestyles.

For instance, a hotel operator may use family-friendly advertising to target a certain demographic by highlighting spacious rooms and fun activities for the whole family. Simultaneously, some business visitors can be eligible for special benefits like early access to company facilities or discounted rates for extended stays.

Managing Language and Cultural Sensitivity: Managing Diversity

In an increasingly global corporate world, businesses must be aware of language and cultural quirks. More than just translation is required for marketing communications to be effectively adapted to varied target audiences; cultural references, conventions, and tastes must also be taken into consideration.

In addition to language barriers, multinational food companies may modify their marketing messaging to account for cultural differences in eating customs, culinary traditions, and taste preferences.

Difficulties and Considerations for Target Audience Segmentation

Balancing Personalization and Privacy Concerns.

Customization improves the user experience, but there is a need to exercise caution while using it, particularly in light of privacy concerns. Businesses must balance giving individualized messages to customers with safeguarding their privacy. Being transparent about data use and offering opt-in options may help to foster trust.

Shifting Market Dynamics and Segment Fluidity.

Customer categorization may change over time due to shifting market conditions. In order to adjust to evolving customer behavior, new trends, and shifting market conditions, businesses need to be adaptable and keep reviewing their segmentation strategy. This necessitates a commitment to ongoing data analysis and research.

Marketing Channel Convergence.

For customers to have a positive experience, marketing channels must remain consistent. Businesses need to make sure that the tailored messages they create for different groups are applied across all channels, including social media, email, websites, and in-person contacts. This integration strengthens the targeted messaging and creates a unified brand image.

Target audience segmentation is essential for marketing strategy from a strategic point of view. By recognizing and understanding the various client types, businesses may more effectively target messages that engage with customers on a personal level. This strengthens ties and increases the effectiveness of marketing campaigns. When businesses embrace the subtleties of each audience and take a multifaceted approach to segmentation, they are better equipped to tackle the complexity of the market with purpose and accuracy. It is not only a prudent strategic move, but it also shows that a company is paying attention to understanding and meeting the unique demands of each and every consumer category, which eventually improves customer satisfaction and fosters long-term business success.

Chapter Five

Choosing the Right Marketing Channels

A thorough analysis of the various marketing channels is necessary to develop an effective marketing plan. In today's fast-paced business world, businesses have a wide range of chances on both conventional and digital platforms. This choice is crucial because it affects a brand's ability to effectively interact with its target audience and the success of all of its marketing initiatives.

Exploring Digital and Traditional Platforms

Online Sources:

Digital marketing is becoming an increasingly important part of today's marketing mix. It is an effective substitute for organizations because to its broad reach and rapid contact abilities. Important components of digital marketing include content marketing, email marketing, search engines, and social media platforms. Each has advantages and disadvantages, and the choice relies on the kind of business and the target market.

Social media sites like as Facebook, Instagram, and Twitter provide a direct line of communication for interacting with customers, increasing brand recognition, and increasing website traffic. Search engine marketing includes paid advertising and search engine optimization (SEO), which guarantee presence when consumers actively look for goods or services. Email marketing with personalized interactions forges enduring relationships with customers. Through blogs, videos, and other media, content marketing establishes credibility and provides value to the audience.

Traditional Locations:

While digital platforms are becoming more and more common, conventional marketing strategies are still useful in certain situations. Print, radio, television, and outdoor advertising are some of the ways to reach certain groups or demographics. It's critical to understand the information consuming habits and media engagement strategies of the target audience.

For instance, small businesses could find success with advertisements in the local newspaper or on the radio, but the best option for reaching a large audience might be television advertising. Events and sponsorships, while they may be more conventional, are effective ways to promote your business. The goal is to strike a balance between conventional and digital media, since the latter may support the former and provide a more comprehensive approach.

Integrated Marketing Approach

A successful marketing campaign often relies on an integrated approach that makes use of the advantages of both conventional and digital media. This synergy ensures better reach and a more cohesive marketing message.

Reliable Branding: It is vital to retain a consistent brand image over all channels. Whether a consumer encounters a company via print advertising, a website, or social media, the language, graphics, and tone should all be the same. This continuity improves brand memory and builds trust.

Data-Driven Decision Making:

A wealth of information available in digital marketing might help inform marketing choices. Metrics like conversion rates, internet traffic, and social media participation may provide valuable information. It may be possible to improve targeting strategies and allocate resources more efficiently by combining this data with conventional market research.

Many Channels of Distribution:

Promoting information and campaigns across a variety of channels increases their effectiveness. For example, a social media campaign may direct users to a website where they may subscribe to an email list. Through several touchpoints, this cross-channel strategy increases the likelihood of conversion for the audience.

Adaptability and Innovation:

An integrated strategy allows for adaptation in the ever-evolving field of marketing. Businesses may test out new channels while maintaining a core presence in well-established ones. This adaptability guarantees that the marketing effort will remain successful and relevant even in the face of shifting customer behavior.

To put it simply, choosing the best marketing channels requires a thorough analysis of both conventional and digital platforms. Traditional channels give a feeling of familiarity and focused reach, whilst digital channels provide immediacy and interaction. When these advantages are combined, an integrated marketing strategy may be more robust and successful. As technology advances, marketers must be flexible, promoting innovation while acknowledging the continued usefulness of tried-and-true strategies.

Chapter Six

Content Strategy

In today's marketing strategies, content plays a crucial role in influencing customer views, brand loyalty, and overall success. A well-thought-out content strategy aims to do more than just provide information; it also connects with readers, engages them, and builds long-lasting relationships. This article addresses the intricacy of content strategy, emphasizing the delivery of informative and engaging material that use narrative techniques.

Creating Engaging and Relevant Content

Aware of the Needs of the Audience:

A thorough understanding of the intended audience is the foundation of every effective content strategy. Marketers must comprehend the concerns, interests, and goals of their audience in order to create content that engages with them. Conducting in-depth market and audience research provides insights into the kinds of products that will really engage customers and improve their lives.

Differing Formats for Media:

When content types are diverse, the brand's message will reach a larger audience. Diverse customer preferences are satisfied by a variety of forms, including blog entries, podcasts, films, infographics, and interactive quizzes. A comprehensive content strategy adapts to the changing digital world to be relevant and accessible across all devices.

Regularity and Regularity:Content must be distributed consistently to keep an audience interested. Establishing a consistent publishing schedule—daily, weekly, or monthly—makes it possible for viewers to anticipate your content. However, regularity shouldn't come at the expense of quality. Each piece of content should be consistent with the brand's values and significantly advance the story overall.

Leveraging Storytelling for Connection

The Power of Storytelling:

Beyond just providing information, storytelling allows the storyteller to connect emotionally with the listener. By telling compelling tales, businesses can connect with customers on a personal level and leave a lasting impression. An engaging story may arouse emotions, inspire confidence, and distinguish a company in a crowded marketplace.

Creating an Ethical Brand:

Using story to highlight a brand's goal, beliefs, and employees may help it become more relevant. These narratives help to define a brand's identity and encourage honesty. They might tell the story of the company's founding, include customer success stories, or highlight employee experiences.

Creating Personas That Are Compelling:

Adding relatable characters to marketing storylines facilitates customer empathy. To accomplish this, you may use user-generated material, testimonials from clients, or fictional characters that represent the company's values. Having relatable personas increases the relatability and approachability of the brand and fosters a sense of community among customers.

Emotional Bonding:

Emotions are a powerful tool for storytelling. A wonderful story may evoke feelings of delight, empathy, nostalgia, or even challenge preconceived notions in listeners. By connecting emotionally with their audience, brands have the potential to leave a lasting impression and increase the shareability and recall value of their content.

Single Tone of Brand:

Maintaining a unified brand voice across all media is essential to achieving coherence in storytelling. Whether a brand goes for a comical, serious, or inspiring tone, it should always be in line with the company's identity. Retaining consistency promotes identification and strengthens the emotional connection that a tale creates.

The Interface Between Narrative and Captivating Content

Synergy between Content and Storytelling:

The most effective content strategies smoothly combine captivating content creation with storytelling. Interesting content is used to convey the brand's story, making it easier for the audience to understand and appreciate.

Story-Based Campaigns:

A consistent brand narrative is produced by organizing marketing initiatives around a single story idea. To keep viewers interested, these advertisements may appear in a variety of mediums. Consistent campaign language improves consumer experience and increases brand awareness.

Interactive Content Experiences:

Interactive content like as surveys, quizzes, and virtual experiences encourage audience participation in the brand's narrative. This improves engagement and tailors the discussion even more. Through interactive content, the audience is transformed from being passive viewers of the brand story to active participants.

Analytics & Metrics:

Both qualitative and quantitative analysis are required to assess the effectiveness of a content strategy. Metrics like as engagement rates, click-through rates, and social share counts provide insight into the efficacy of content. Customer feedback and sentiment monitoring may also be used to gauge the emotional impact of narrative.

Success in the ever-evolving world of marketing depends on having a strong content strategy. Brands may establish strong relationships with their audience by using storytelling to provide interesting and relevant content. This two-pronged approach draws attention while simultaneously encouraging brand loyalty and advocacy, ensuring that the business retains a substantial presence in customers' hearts and minds.

Chapter Seven

Budgeting and Resource Allocation

A marketing strategy's budget and resource distribution are critical factors that impact a campaign's likelihood of success and endurance. Marketers have to allocate costs efficiently and maximize return on investment (ROI) with the limited resources at their disposal. This article explores methods for delving into the complexities of resource allocation and budgeting in order to maximize spending and provide quantifiable rewards.

Allocating Resources Effectively

Aware of Your Promotional Channels

Before spending any money, marketers must have a thorough understanding of every marketing channel that is accessible. Each channel, whether it digital platforms like social media, search engine marketing, and content marketing, or conventional channels like print, radio, and events, has unique benefits and caters to different audience groups. Analyzing the target market and the characteristics of the product or service is necessary to identify the best channels for contacting prospective clients.

Activities with High Impact Are Prioritized:

Every marketing initiative is not made equal. Marketers must create high-impact initiatives that support organizational goals. This may include carefully examining previous campaigns to see what worked and to understand the factors that made them successful. Setting projects with a proven track record at the top of the priority list allows resources to be allocated where they will most likely produce positive results.

Combining Paid and Organic Methods Strategically:

In the digital world, there has to be a link made between paid and organic techniques. While paid advertising offers quick awareness, organic initiatives like content marketing and search engine optimization (SEO) contribute to long-term sustainability. By appropriately balancing various tactics, it is possible to maintain a comprehensive marketing plan that optimizes both short-term growth and long-term income.

Customization Strategies for Target Segments:

Different target segments need different amounts of funding. It is possible to optimize resources when marketing strategies are tailored to the characteristics and behaviors of certain target audiences. When the message, material, and promotional activities are specifically designed to appeal to each demographic, the campaign's overall efficacy is increased.

Maximizing ROI in Marketing Initiatives

Selecting Particular Objectives:

To optimize return on investment, marketers must set clear, quantifiable goals for every marketing campaign. Whether the aim is to increase revenue, improve website traffic, or build brand recognition, a framework for resource allocation is provided by having well-defined goals. SMART stands for specific, measurable, attainable, time-bound, and defined goals.

Data-Driven Decision Making:

In the digital age, a marketer's most valuable resource is data. Analytics technologies facilitate the tracking of key performance indicators (KPIs), enabling data-driven decision-making. Marketers has the ability to evaluate which campaigns, channels, or strategies provide the best outcomes and allocate resources accordingly. Regular review and adjustments based on data insights improve the overall effectiveness of marketing campaigns.

Assessment and Practice:

It is crucial to foster a culture of testing and iteration in order to maximize return on investment. Marketers should embrace A/B testing in order to evaluate ad creatives, message, and targeting criteria. Marketers may discover what appeals to their target audience the most via iterative testing and plan refinement, which ultimately results in more effective budget allocation.

Metrics for Counterpartum Acquisition (CPA):

The cost per acquisition is one of the most important metrics for evaluating the effectiveness of marketing efforts. By dividing the entire cost of a campaign by the quantity of new clients it has acquired, marketers may determine how cost-effective a campaign is. When CPA is tracked and optimized, resources are allocated to the projects with the lowest acquisition costs.

Aligning Budget with Business Goals

Dividing Up Funds by Priority:

As soon as goals and objectives are established, the financial aspect of resource management becomes crucial. Allocate resources based on the importance of each campaign's contribution to the company's objectives. It can be more appropriate to allocate funds to high-priority projects that directly impact revenue or brand positioning.

Readiness for Novel Opportunities:

While preparation is essential, budgetary flexibility allows marketers to seize new possibilities. Market dynamics, industry trends, and consumer behavior are all subject to sudden shifts. A flexible budget ensures that resources are allocated to the most successful areas and enables marketers to respond quickly to unanticipated opportunities or obstacles.

Distinctive and Prolonged Budgeting:

Effective planning takes into account both short-term profits and long-term sustainability. Spend money on both short-term and long-term advertising campaigns that can help build your brand and foster client loyalty. A holistic strategy enhances the overall effect of the marketing budget by striking a balance between long-term expenditures and short-term goals.

Creating a budget and allocating resources are essential elements of a successful marketing plan. For the best use of resources, it is crucial to have a firm understanding of target audiences, to prioritize high-impact initiatives, and to modify approaches for different market groups. Optimizing return on investment requires setting clear goals, using data to inform decisions, and creating a culture of testing and iteration. If marketers maintain their budgets flexible and aligned with corporate objectives, they may effectively traverse the always evolving landscape of marketing. This aids in optimizing their endeavors for sustained prosperity and numerical outcomes.

Chapter Eight

Implementation Plan

A well-thought-out marketing strategy's effectiveness depends on how it is implemented. The implementation plan serves as a guide to help turn strategic ideas into tangible outcomes. The primary elements of implementing a marketing strategy are covered in this article, with special emphasis placed on the need for a well-thought-out implementation plan and the ongoing process of monitoring and optimizing tactics for best results.

Executing the Marketing Strategy

Unambiguous Coordination and Communication: The cornerstones of execution are good collaboration and communication across the whole company. All personnel involved in carrying out the marketing plan, even executives at the top, must be conscious of their own responsibilities. Keeping the lines of communication open guarantees that everyone in the team is on the same page about the overall aims and objectives.

Detailed Timetable and Comparisons: A comprehensive schedule with designated checkpoints should be included in an implementation strategy. The execution process is structured by the establishment of deadlines and the division of the plan into manageable sections. This timetable serves as a roadmap to help the team stay responsible and focused on the current tasks at hand.

Resource Allocation and Budget Management: For effective execution, resource allocation must be done appropriately. Make sure that teams have the tools, resources, and instruction needed to carry out their responsibilities. To prevent overpaying and ensure that existing funds are allocated in accordance with the objectives of the marketing plan, vigilant budget management is also necessary.

The way in which cross-functions interact: Departmental collaboration is a key element of modern marketing strategies. Cross-functional cooperation creates a comprehensive strategy where several teams pool their knowledge to accomplish shared objectives. Whether in sales, marketing alignment, customer service, or product development, collaboration boosts the strategy's overall efficacy.

Technology Integration: Technology use is essential to a job well done. Technology, such as Customer Relationship Management (CRM) systems, marketing automation tools, and analytics platforms, facilitates the execution of many processes and provides critical insights. Efficiency is increased and data-driven decision-making becomes possible by incorporating these technologies into the process.

Monitoring and Adjusting Techniques

Cognitive Information:

Analytics that are updated in real time are essential for tracking the success of marketing campaigns. Use data analytics technologies to monitor key performance indicators (KPIs) and discover more about the efficacy of different initiatives. This real-time feedback loop helps marketers identify new trends and quickly modify their strategies in response to changing customer behavior.

Key performance indicators, or KPIs: Establishing and tracking KPIs is essential to success monitoring. KPIs vary based on the specific objectives of the marketing plan. Whether increasing conversion rates, lead creation, brand awareness, or client retention is the goal, creating and regularly tracking KPIs provides a concrete measure of success.

Input and Engagement from Clients:

When it comes to monitoring operations, qualitative data from consumer feedback is equally as useful as quantitative ones. To actively engage consumers and get insights into their experiences, make use of social media, surveys, and direct communication. This input might help pinpoint areas that need improvement and guide changes to improve the overall customer experience.

A Competitive Analysis:

The marketing environment is dynamic, and rivals may modify their strategies. Regularly do competition analysis to stay abreast of market developments, emerging technologies, and shifting customer preferences. Comparing performance metrics with rivals gives context for changes in tactics and helps maintain a competitive advantage.

Technical Method:

Adopting an agile approach is essential to keep up with the ever evolving marketing landscape. Strive for adaptability rather than fervently adhering to one strategy. Agile marketing is known for its iterative cycles, which allow teams to test and learn from approaches, make data-driven adjustments, and continuously improve performance.

Continuous Improvement and Adjustment

Post-Campaign Evaluation:

After specific campaigns or initiatives are implemented, carry out in-depth post-campaign assessments. Analyze the outcomes in the context of the stated goals, emphasize any achievements and potential areas for development, and create a report on the lessons learned. This retrospective study helps shape future tactics and fosters a culture of continuous development.

Group Education and Feedback Cycles:

Establish channels for the marketing team members to provide feedback. Regular team meetings, knowledge-sharing exercises, and productive criticism sessions may foster a culture of learning. It is important to support team members in discussing problems, exchanging ideas, and developing creative solutions. Collaborative learning increases the team's capacity for long-term growth and adaptability.

Iterative Strategies Refined:

A marketing plan should evolve over time in response to market dynamics, customer behavior, and performance data. Regularly review and modify the overall plan while taking new possibilities and challenges into account. Iterative strategies guarantee that the marketing plan stays aligned with corporate objectives and flexible enough to change with the business environment.

Implementing a marketing strategy is a dynamic process that requires careful preparation, effective communication, and strategic cooperation. Achieving success requires completing every phase, from the original implementation plan to ongoing strategy adjustments and monitoring. Establishing a culture of agility, data-driven decision-making, and continuous development may help marketing teams succeed in the long run. Teams may accomplish short-term objectives and successfully traverse the difficult marketing climate with the aid of this strategy.

Chapter Nine

Metrics and Analytics

Metrics and analytics, which provide crucial insights into audience behavior, performance, and overall effectiveness, are the foundation of every successful marketing campaign. This article discusses the importance of key performance indicators (KPIs), the need for a thorough understanding of these measurements, and the strategic use of analytics to gauge a marketing campaign's effectiveness.

Key performance indicators, or KPIs

Definitions of KPIs

Key performance indicators, or KPIs, are quantitative measurements that are used to assess how well a marketing plan is doing in relation to certain attributes. These assessments provide a clear picture of how strategic objectives are developing since they serve as benchmarks. The KPI selection process is significantly impacted by the marketing strategy's stated goals.

Choosing Relevant KPIs: Good KPIs shouldn't be a one-size-fits-all approach; instead, they should be tailored to the specific objectives of the marketing plan. For example, if increasing brand recognition is the main goal, KPIs related to social media reach, website traffic, or impressions may be included. KPIs for lead creation might include conversion rates, click-through rates, and the quantity of qualified leads.

Models of Marketing KPIs

1. Conversion Rate: The proportion of visitors to a website that finish an intended activity, such as making a purchase or filling out a form.

2. The Amount Spent on Acquiring a New Customer (CAC): Is the result of dividing marketing expenses by the quantity of new customers acquired.

3. Return on Investment (ROI): The ratio of net profit to marketing investment cost expressed as a percentage.

4. Click-Through Rate (CTR): This refers to the proportion of viewers that clicked on an advertisement or link.

5. The projected net profit related to the duration of a customer's future relationship is known as Customer Lifetime Value (CLV).

Measuring the Success of Your Strategy

Selecting Particular Objectives:
The marketing plan must include clear aims before focusing on metrics and statistics. SMART stands for specific, measurable, attainable, time-bound, and defined goals. The first stage in creating relevant KPIs and evaluating progress toward predetermined objectives is to create clear goals.

Metric Alignment with Corporate Goals: Measurements and analytics should be clearly aligned with overarching company objectives. If the organization's primary goal is to increase revenue, then marketing metrics should concentrate on components that help generate cash, such as conversion rates and client acquisition costs. This partnership guarantees that marketing initiatives are strategically advancing the company's expansion.

Continuous Surveillance and Reporting: Some key performance indicators need to be routinely checked in order to remain informed about ongoing performance. Marketing teams may monitor advancements, identify patterns, and anticipate possible challenges by establishing a consistent reporting framework. Regular or real-time reports provide the information required to make wise decisions and enable quick adjustments to the plan of action when necessary.

Comparative Evaluation: By providing context for performance measurements, comparative analysis enables success evaluation that transcends simple numerical values. A point of comparison may be obtained by setting benchmarks against rival companies, industry norms, or historical data. It is necessary to assess trends over time and compare outcomes with predetermined benchmarks in order to determine if the marketing plan is succeeding or failing to meet its goals.

Correcting for Client Feedback: Customer feedback, both quantitative and qualitative, is a factor in success measurement. Social media interactions, reviews, and surveys may all provide insight into the attitude and contentment of customers. Marketers may ensure that their strategy speaks to and meets the requirements and preferences of their target audience by adapting their approaches in response to this data.

Gaining Strategic Understanding using Analytics

Innovative Analytical Tools:

Sophisticated analytics technologies are readily available to marketers nowadays. These platforms provide a variety of data, including Google Analytics, social media analytics, and customer relationship management (CRM) systems. The most difficult component is locating important information in this data to improve strategic decision-making.

Attribution for Modeling:

By using attribution modeling, marketers may get a deeper understanding of the customer journey and assign conversions to important touchpoints. Whether it's an email campaign, blog post, or social media marketing, attribution modeling gives you insight into the channels that result in the biggest conversions. The allocation and optimization of resources are guided by this information.

Semantic Forecast:

Predictive analytics makes predictions about future patterns and behaviors based on historical data. By looking for connections and patterns in data, marketers may forecast likely outcomes. Predictive analytics is especially useful for the goals of proactive problem-solving, marketing optimization, and consumer behavior prediction.

Optimization using A/B Testing: A/B testing, also referred to as split testing, compares two iterations of a website, advertisement, or other marketing piece to see which works better. Marketers may improve headlines, images, calls-to-action, and other elements by using this technique. Marketers may optimize their approaches for maximum efficacy by doing comprehensive testing and analyzing the results.

Analytics and metrics serve as the strategy's compass in marketing. Key Performance Indicators (KPIs) function like traffic signals, indicating the direction and speed of advancement toward predetermined goals. The effectiveness of a marketing plan can only be determined by carefully selecting the appropriate criteria, linking it to organizational objectives, and pledging to undergo ongoing assessment and modification.

By using predictive analytics, attribution modeling, and advanced analytics technologies, marketers may get a deeper understanding of consumer behavior and market dynamics. A culture that prioritizes regular reporting, comparative analysis, and adaption based on customer input ensures that the marketing plan is adaptable and flexible enough to take advantage of changing opportunities and overcome challenges.

In the dynamic world of marketing, success is not a static state but rather an ongoing process of developing, optimizing, and fine-tuning strategies based on analytics and metrics data.

Chapter Ten

Adaptation and Evolution

Maintaining a Flexible Attitude in the Face of a Changing Market: Being flexible is not only a strategy, but also a need in the fast-paced marketing sector. The dynamic nature of client behavior, technological progress, and industry shifts need flexible and adaptive marketing techniques for optimal effectiveness. Agile marketing is all about being nimble enough to react quickly to changes, grab opportunities, and make real-time revisions to marketing strategies based on data.

Programs That Encourage Participation: A thorough grasp of the intended audience is essential for any adaptation to be successful. Marketing professionals are able to react with campaigns that are relevant to the current state of the industry by analyzing data and keeping an eye on customer behavior. Being adaptable refers to the capacity to swiftly change and fit in with the changing surroundings, no matter what the cause—a change in consumer preferences or the introduction of a new trend, for example.

Thank You for Using Technology: Technological innovations are catalysts for change. It is essential for marketers to be abreast of the latest technology developments, including social media algorithms and expanding digital platforms. Innovative technologies may provide businesses a competitive edge and increase client satisfaction in marketing initiatives.

Iterative Strategy Improvement: Iterative method refining requires ongoing instruction, testing, and modification. Using this iterative cycle, marketers may improve campaigns based on performance data. Developing an attitude of continuous improvement guarantees that marketing strategies respond to the market's ever-evolving dynamics.

Case Studies: Real-World Examples of Successful Marketing Strategies

Examining actual events provides insightful knowledge about effective marketing strategies and the ideas that support them.

1. Nike's "Just Do It" campaign: Mirroring social values, this classic Nike campaign went beyond conventional marketing. Nike created a strong emotional connection with its customers by associating the brand with motivational ideas, which helped to build brand loyalty.

2. Apple Product Launches: Apple's product introductions set the standard for customer interaction and anticipation. Through meticulous event planning, the company generates buzz and an air of exclusivity that drives demand.

3. Dollar Shave Club's Creative Marketing: Dollar Shave Club revolutionized the razor industry by taking a daring, lighthearted, and cost-effective strategy. By using internet platforms and viral marketing, the company quickly increased its market share, demonstrating the effectiveness of creative marketing techniques.

Regarding Matters Legal and Ethical: Overcoming Marketing Ethics:

Ethics must be taken into account in sustainable marketing strategies. Maintaining ethical standards and earning the confidence of customers is not only morally right, but also practically necessary. Important concerns include ethics, customer privacy, and transparency.

Marketing Transparency: Sincerity and honesty in advertising increase credibility. Being open and honest about a product's features, advantages, and potential drawbacks is essential to establishing trust. Deceptive business practices undermine customer confidence and may have a lasting negative impact on a brand's image.

Data Security and Privacy: As the reliance on data-driven activities grows, customer data protection becomes more important. Adhering to data privacy standards and putting strong security measures in place ensures consumer security and legal compliance.

Corporate Responsibility: Consumer awareness of a business's social responsibility is rising. Marketing tactics that promote ethical behavior, environmental sustainability, and social issues tend to attract clientele that are socially aware. Brands that really improve society have stronger, more enduring relationships with their target market.

Compliance with Regulations

Marketers need to navigate the legal landscape in order to remain reliable and avoid any legal issues.

GDPR and Data Protection: The General Data Protection Regulation (GDPR) has significantly changed how businesses manage client data. Marketing initiatives that use customer data are required to ensure adherence to the GDPR and other data protection regulations.

Truths About Advertising Law: There are strict guidelines governing the integrity of advertising in different locations. Marketers must adhere to these guidelines and ensure that any claims they make in their advertisements are supported by evidence. Failure to comply may result in legal ramifications and harm to the brand's image.

Industry-Specific Regulations: Different businesses may have unique restrictions pertaining to marketing techniques. Marketers must be knowledgeable about industry-specific standards in order to prevent breaking any rules.

Robust marketing tactics are based on the fundamental concepts of evolution, flexibility, and moral reasoning. To be flexible in a market that is evolving, one must continuously learn, adjust to change, and be open to new ideas. Case studies from real-world situations provide crucial insights into the tactics that have successfully connected with audiences.

A marketing plan cannot jeopardize its adherence to morality and the law. Maintaining moral principles fosters customer trust, which contributes to a company's long-term viability. Keeping an eye on the legal landscape guarantees that marketing campaigns are both successful and compliant with industry standards.

Strategies that prioritize adaptability, ongoing improvement, moral dilemmas, and legal compliance prosper in the dynamic marketing landscape and create enduring relationships with customers.

Conclusion

A strong marketing strategy is, in essence, a delicate ballet that requires a well-balanced combination of moral awareness, inventiveness, and flexibility. Instead of being a static blueprint, an effective marketing strategy is a dynamic roadmap that navigates the always changing landscape of customer behavior, market dynamics, and technology breakthroughs.

In this study on marketing strategy, we have taken into account crucial elements that lead to success. Every element—from the laborious process of selecting the best marketing channels to the skill of building a narrative that forges enduring connections—is essential to developing a plan that connects with the target audience.

Budgeting and resource allocation, which ensure that resources are deployed effectively to optimize return on investment, are the financial foundation of a marketing plan. The execution plan, which emphasizes the need for precise timelines, effective communication, and technological integration, gives the strategic visions life.

For marketers, analytics and metrics serve as a compass that helps them gauge the success of their campaigns. Key Performance Indicators (KPIs) are metrics that show how well a certain goal is being achieved. Using analytics tools, using attribution modeling, and implementing predictive analytics are all components of a data-driven strategy that improves performance via plan modification.

Evolution and adaptation become crucial in a dynamic economy. Being agile includes using technology, adapting quickly to changes, and continuously improving methods. Real-world case studies provide concrete examples of effective strategies, providing educational and inspirational insights for marketers who want to pick the brains of industry leaders.

Adherence to regulations and ethical dilemmas highlight the need of integrity in marketing strategy. Upholding moral principles fosters customer trust, while adhering to the law protects the brand's reputation and durability.

Simply said, a strong marketing strategy is a tapestry made of creativity, data-driven decision-making, and moral commitment. It's a journey that calls for continual adaptation, flexibility, and a thorough understanding of the ever-changing demands and preferences of the target audience.

As the marketing landscape continues to change, successful marketers will be those that welcome change, learn from their successes and failures, and never waver from their dedication to forging deep relationships with their target audience. One strategy ends and a new one begins as the cycle of moral innovation, improvement, and adaptation drives businesses toward long-term success in the dynamic field of marketing.